WHY MIRABEAU LAMAR MATTERS TO TEXAS

By Robin Johnson

Published in 2014 by The Rosen Publishing Group, Inc.
29 East 21st Street, New York, NY 10010

First Edition

Developed, written, and produced by Digital Discovery Publishing
Editors: Molly Aloian, Wendy Scavuzzo
Design & Production: Katherine Berti
Curriculum & content coordinator: Reagan Miller
Photo research: Crystal Sikkens, Allison Napier
Proofreader: Sarah Cairns

Photo Credits: Digital Discovery Publishing
The Bridgeman Library: The Stapleton Collection: 14 (bottom)
The Granger Collection, NYC: 7 (bottom), 20, 21, 26
Courtesy of Lamar University: 29
Library of Congress: 27
North Wind Picture Archives: 1, 4, 8 (bottom), 13, 25
San Jacinto Museum of History: 28
Shutterstock: 2, 5, 6, 11
Tarlton Law Library, University of Texas at Austin: 19
Texas State Library and Archives Commission: 8 (top), 9, 14 (top), 15, 16, 17, 22
Texas State Preservation Board: cover, 18
Univeristy of North Texas Libraries, Denton, Texas: 24
Wikimedia Commons: 7 (top), 10, 12, 23, 30
Maps by Digital Discovery Publishing: 5, 6, 11

All websites were live and accurate at the time of printing.

Library of Congress Cataloging-in-Publication Data

Johnson, Robin.
Why Mirabeau Lamar matters to Texas / by Robin Johnson.
p. cm. – (Texas perspectives)
Includes index.
ISBN 978-1-4777-0915-3 (library binding) – ISBN 978-1-4777-0939-9 (pbk.) – ISBN 978-1-4777-0940-5 (6-pack)
1. Lamar, Mirabeau Buonaparte, 1798-1859 – Juvenile literature. 2. Presidents – Texas – Biography – Juvenile literature. 3. Texas – Politics and government – To 1846 – Juvenile literature. 4. Texas – History – Republic, 1836-1846 – Juvenile literature. I. Title.
F390.L2 J66 2013
976.4'04–dc23

Manufactured in the United States of America

CPSIA Compliance Information: Batch W13PK: For Further Information contact Rosen Publishing, New York, New York at 1-800-237-9932

CONTENTS

1 THE POET PRESIDENT

When Mirabeau Buonaparte Lamar was born, his family must have dreamed he would one day become a powerful man. Mirabeau was a determined leader and brave freedom fighter. He fought for Texas almost from the moment he moved there. Like his family, Mirabeau Lamar had big dreams.

SOUTHERN GENTLEMAN

Mirabeau was born and raised in Georgia. He was a romantic southern gentleman who often wrote poetry. He used his poems to express his feelings about love, death, war, and other parts of his life. He was called "the Poet President." Mirabeau was also a **scholar** who knew the importance of education. As the president of the Republic of Texas, he set out to create a public school system. His efforts earned him the nickname "Father of Texas Education."

▼ *Mirabeau Lamar was named after Comte de Mirabeau and Napoleon Bonaparte, two powerful men from France who fought for their country's freedom.*

From a letter Mirabeau Lamar wrote on February 23, 1842:

"...it is true when I say that I have never seen the hour since my arrival in Texas, that I have not been willing to sacrifice my life to the glory and happiness of the people. It was for this that I came to the country."

FEARLESS LEADER

Mirabeau led his men to victory on the battlefields. He also led the republic as both president and vice president. When Mirabeau became president in 1838, Texas had no money and a lot of problems. That did not stop Mirabeau. He was determined to grow Texas into a strong, safe, and **prosperous** nation. His plans sometimes failed, but Mirabeau Lamar never stopped fighting for the country he believed in.

Texas Perspective

Mirabeau had three main goals. He wanted to expand Texas into an empire, expand the armed forces, and create public schools.

MIRABEAU LAMAR'S TEXAS

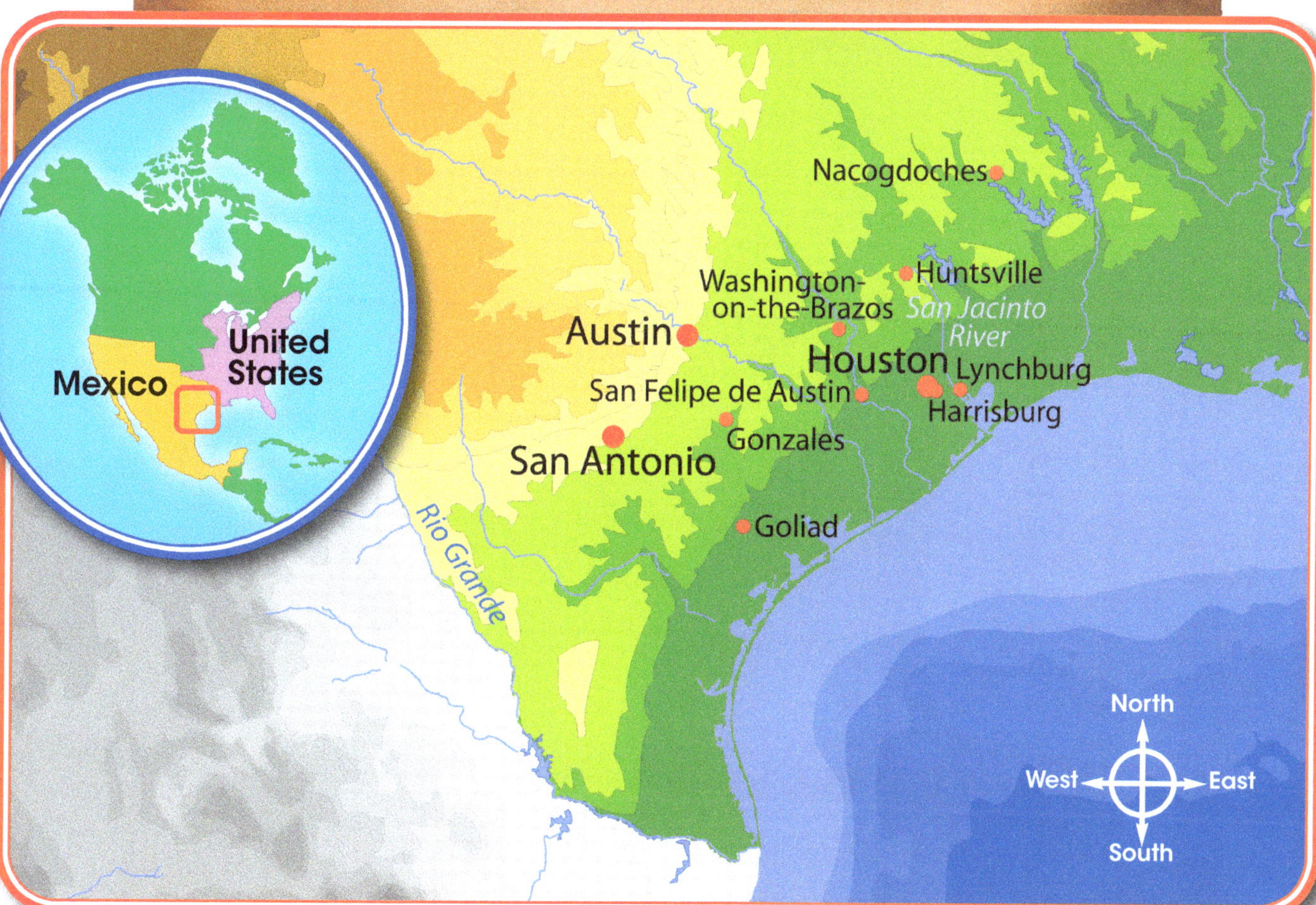

2 GEORGIA ROOTS

Mirabeau Lamar was born on August 16, 1798, near Louisville, Georgia. He grew up near Milledgeville on his father's plantation. A plantation is a large farm on which people live and work. Mirabeau's family was very successful and held a high place in Georgia society.

LIVING LARGE

Mirabeau came from a large, close-knit family. He had four brothers and five sisters. Like many families in the South, Mirabeau's family owned slaves. They had about 50 African-American slaves who worked for them on their 1,000-acre (405 ha) farm. Mirabeau had a fine home and went to good schools. He studied hard and was very creative. He enjoyed reading, oil painting, and writing poems. Mirabeau was also athletic. He became a skilled horseback rider and fencer. These skills would serve him well later in life.

When Mirabeau was 21, he left Georgia to make his mark on the world. He moved to Cahawba, which was the capital of Alabama at the time. There, he helped run a general store and a newspaper called the Cahawba Press.

FIRST STEPS

In 1823, Mirabeau moved back home to Georgia and began his career in **politics**. He worked as the secretary for George Troup, the governor of Georgia. Troup was trying to remove Creek Indians from the state. Like many Americans, he wanted Indians off the land so Anglo Americans could settle there. Mirabeau toured the country and gave speeches for the governor. He also took on the governor's beliefs about Indian removal. Those beliefs would later shape Mirabeau's decisions as

George Troup was governor of Georgia from 1823 until 1827.

INDIAN REMOVAL

In 1803, the United States bought a huge area of land from France. The deal was called the Louisiana Purchase. Soon American pioneers began moving west to settle the land. Indians were already living there, however, so the Americans tried to get the Indians off the land. In 1830, the United States passed a law called the Indian Removal Act. The law allowed Americans to **negotiate** with Indians for their lands. Many thousands of Indians were forced to move to an area west of the Mississippi River called Indian Territory.

The sad journey of Indian removal became known as the Trail of Tears.

FAMILY MAN

During his travels, Mirabeau met Tabitha Jordan. Tabitha was a beautiful but frail young woman. The couple was married on January 1, 1826. The following year, they had a daughter named Rebecca Ann. The young family moved to Columbus, Georgia, in 1828. There, Mirabeau started a newspaper called the *Columbus Enquirer*. In 1829, he was elected to the Georgia Senate. With a new family and a promising career, it should have been a happy time for Lamar.

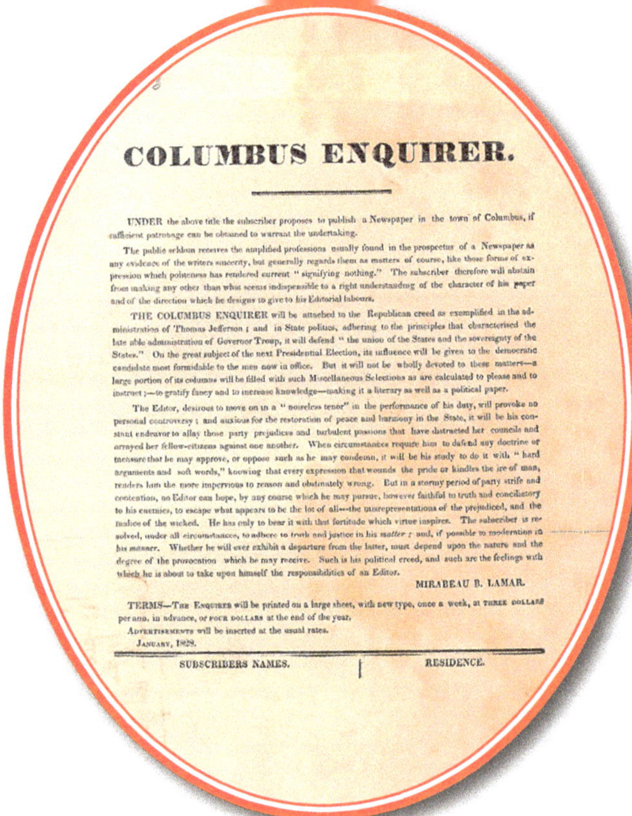

COLUMBUS ENQUIRER.

UNDER the above title the subscriber proposes to publish a Newspaper in the town of Columbus, if sufficient patronage can be obtained to warrant the undertaking.

The public seldom receives the amplified professions usually found in the prospectus of a Newspaper as any evidence of the writers sincerity, but generally regards them as matters of course, like those forms of expression which politeness has rendered current "signifying nothing." The subscriber therefore will abstain from making any other than what seems indispensible to a right understanding of the character of his paper and of the direction which he designs to give to his Editorial labours.

THE COLUMBUS ENQUIRER will be attached to the Republican creed as exemplified in the administration of Thomas Jefferson; and in State politics, adhering to the principles that characterised the late able administration of Governor Troup, it will defend "the union of the States and the sovereignty of the States." On the great subject of the next Presidential Election, its influence will be given to the democratic candidate most formidable to the men now in office. But it will not be wholly devoted to these matters—a large portion of its columns will be filled with such Miscellaneous Selections as are calculated to please and to instruct;—to gratify fancy and to increase knowledge—making it a literary as well as a political paper.

The Editor, desirous to move on in a "noiseless tenor" in the performance of his duty, will provoke no personal controversy; and anxious for the restoration of peace and harmony in the State, it will be his constant endeavor to allay those party prejudices and turbulent passions that have distracted her councils and arrayed her fellow-citizens against one another. When circumstances require him to defend any doctrine or measure that he may approve, or oppose such as he may condemn, it will be his study to do it with "hard arguments and soft words," knowing that every expression that wounds the pride or kindles the ire of man, renders him the more impervious to reason and obstinately wrong. But in a stormy period of party strife and contention, no Editor can hope, by any course which he may pursue, however faithful to truth and conciliatory to his enemies, to escape what appears to be the lot of all—the misrepresentations of the prejudiced, and the malice of the wicked. He has only to bear it with that fortitude which virtue inspires. The subscriber is resolved, under all circumstances, to adhere to truth and justice in his *matter*; and, if possible to moderation in his *manner*. Whether he will ever exhibit a departure from the latter, must depend upon the nature and the degree of the provocation which he may receive. Such is his political creed, and such are the feelings with which he is about to take upon himself the responsibilities of an Editor.

MIRABEAU B. LAMAR.

TERMS—THE ENQUIRER will be printed on a large sheet, with new type, once a week, at THREE DOLLARS per ann. in advance, or FOUR DOLLARS at the end of the year.

ADVERTISEMENTS will be inserted at the usual rates.

JANUARY, 1828.

SUBSCRIBERS NAMES.	RESIDENCE.

▲ *Mirabeau put together a plan to start a newspaper called the* Columbus Enquirer.

LOST LOVE

Sadly, Tabitha soon became ill with a disease called **tuberculosis**. Mirabeau cared for his sick wife until she died in 1830 at the age of 21. Mirabeau was heartbroken. He left his young daughter to be raised by an aunt and uncle. He also left public life to travel and write poetry.

Mirabeau created some of his best-known poems during the sad time of his life after his wife died. The poems included "Thou Idol of My Soul" and "At Evening on the Banks of the Chattahoochee."

REBECCA LAMAR

Mirabeau loved his daughter Rebecca dearly. Although he did not raise Rebecca, the two were very close. They wrote letters and visited one another often. Sadly, Rebecca died when she was just 15 years old.

Rebecca Lamar was named after Mirabeau's mother, who died in 1839.

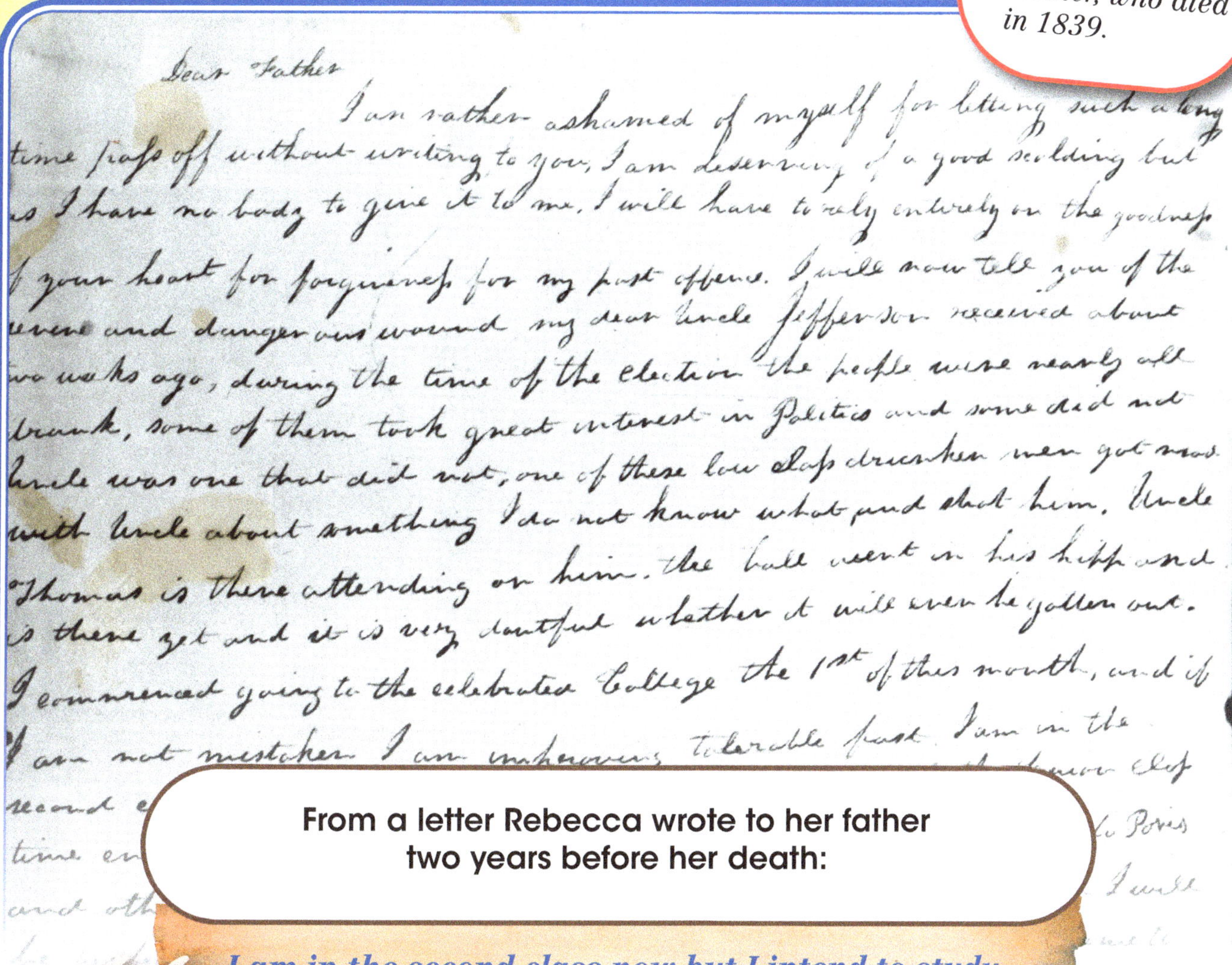

Dear Father

I am rather ashamed of myself for letting such a long time pass off without writing to you, I am deserving of a good scolding but as I have no body to give it to me, I will have to rely entirely on the goodness of your heart for forgiveness for my past offence. I will now tell you of the severe and dangerous wound my dear Uncle Jefferson received about two weeks ago, during the time of the election the people were nearly all drunk, some of them took great interest in Politics and some did not Uncle was one that did not, one of these low class drunken men got mad with Uncle about something I do not know what and shot him. Uncle Thomas is there attending on him. the ball went in his hipp and is there yet and it is very doubtful whether it will ever be gotten out. I commenced going to the celebrated College the 1st of this month, and if I am not mistaken I am improving tolerable fast. I am in the second c...

From a letter Rebecca wrote to her father two years before her death:

> *I am in the second class now but I intend to study hard and get in the Senior class in time enough to graduate in about two years! Then I am going to Paris and other cities and continue travelling two years and then I will be perfectly satisfied to remain with you always if you will come to the United States.*

MORE SADNESS

In 1832, Mirabeau Lamar ran for a seat in the US **Congress**. He was not elected. The next year, he passed the bar exam to become a lawyer. He ran for Congress again in 1834, but again he was not elected. Then tragedy struck Mirabeau again. His brother Lucius killed himself. Mirabeau had been very close to his brother and was overcome with sadness. He left Georgia and traveled to Texas. It was a decision that would change his life forever.

Lucius Quintus Cincinnatus Lamar II was Mirabeau's nephew. He was very young when his father killed himself. He later became a justice on the Supreme Court of the United States.

THE STATE OF TEXAS

In the 1820s, Texas belonged to Mexico. It was a wild, unsettled area of land just west of the American border. Few people lived in Texas at the time, so Texas was joined to another Mexican state called Coahuila. The new Mexican state was renamed Coahuila y Tejas, which is Spanish for Coahuila and Texas.

The Mexican government wanted to fill the new territory with people, so Mexico let people from other countries claim land there. Thousands of Anglo-American settlers from the United States began moving to Texas to get land and build homes. The settlers did not always obey the laws of their new country. Many brought slaves with them to work on their ranches and in their cotton fields. It was illegal to own slaves in Mexico at the time.

In 1830, the Mexican government made new laws to stop Americans with slaves from moving to Mexico. The Mexican government built forts and put soldiers around the country to keep Americans out. In 1835, Mexican president Antonio López de Santa Anna took control of the country. Santa Anna was a powerful **dictator** who used the Mexican army to control his people. Many Texas settlers did not agree with the new laws and new form of government. The settlers began to **revolt** against Mexico.

This map shows the state of Coahuila and Texas in 1825. Many settlers wanted Texas to be a separate state within the country of Mexico.

3 THE TEXAS REVOLUTION

When Mirabeau arrived in Texas in 1835, the Texas Revolution had just begun. It was a war between the Mexican government and Texas settlers. The settlers were fighting for their independence. Mexican president Santa Anna wanted to keep control of his people.

BATTLE OF GONZALES

The Texas Revolution started with the Battle of Gonzales on October 2, 1835. The Mexican army had given a cannon to the settlers of Gonzales, Texas, to protect their town against Indian attacks. When Texans began to revolt, the Mexican army tried to take back the cannon. Texan settlers did not let them take it, and they won the Battle of Gonzales. It was a small but important victory for Texas.

WHO WAS JAMES FANNIN?

James Walker Fannin Jr. was born in Georgia in 1804. In 1834, he settled in Velasco, Texas. He owned a plantation and worked in the slave trade there. He also became a leader of the Texas Revolution. Fannin wrote letters asking for money and men to fight for Texas. He also served in the volunteer army. He fought at the Battle of Gonzales and the Battle of Concepción. He was soon promoted to colonel in the regular army. Fannin and his men stormed a Mexican fort, called Presidio La Bahia, in the town of Goliad. The Texans took control of the fort and renamed it Fort **Defiance**.

Mirabeau visited his old friend James Fannin in Texas. He decided to join the war Fannin and other brave Texans were fighting.

THE ALAMO

The Texas Revolution lasted for more than six months. During that time, many deadly battles took place. On February 23, 1836, Mexican troops gathered near a Texas fort called the Alamo. After two weeks of minor **skirmishes** between the forces, the Mexican army attacked. On March 6, about 1,800 Mexican soldiers stormed the Alamo. Only 189 Texan soldiers defended the fort.

In less than 90 minutes of fighting, about 600 Mexican soldiers were killed or wounded. Nearly all the Texan soldiers died in battle. A few Texans surrendered and were **executed** by Santa Anna's men. The brutal battle and the cruelty of Santa Anna caused many Texans to join the army.

"Remember the Alamo!" became a battle cry for Texas soldiers.

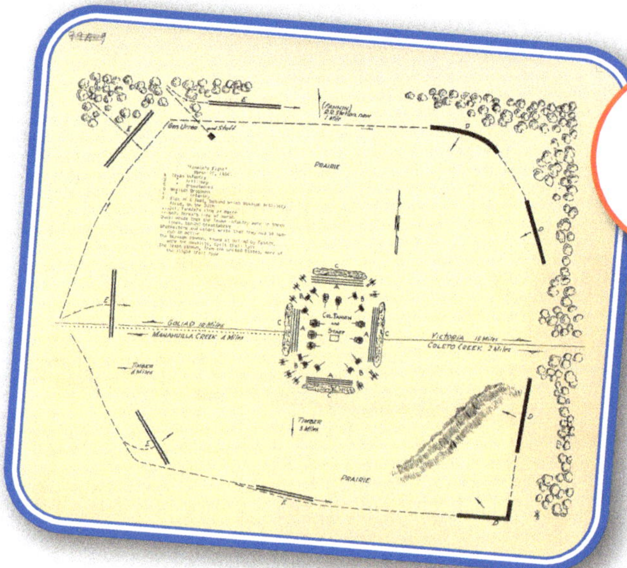

The Battle of Coleto, shown in this sketch, ended with the capture of James Fannin and his men.

JOINING THE FIGHT

Mirabeau rushed back to Georgia. He sold his part of the *Columbus Enquirer*. He got money from his brothers to buy land in Texas. Then he packed his belongings and returned to Texas to join Fannin in the fight for freedom. When he arrived in Texas, Mirabeau found out that his friend had been killed at the Goliad **Massacre**.

THE GOLIAD MASSACRE

On March 19, 1836, the Mexican army attacked James Fannin and his troops as they were leaving Presidio La Bahia, or Fort Defiance as James Fannin called it. The troops fought the two-day Battle of Coleto. The Texans surrendered and were taken back to the fort as prisoners of war. Mexican president Santa Anna ordered his soldiers to kill all the prisoners.

On March 27, Fannin and about 340 Texan soldiers were lined up and shot outside the fort. This became known as the Goliad Massacre.

From the letter Mirabeau wrote to his brother Jefferson on April 10, 1836:

"I leave in the morning for the army; a dreadful Battle is to be fought in three or four days, [to decide] the fate of Texas; I shall of course have to be in it...Fannin's Army is entirely lost...They were kept prisoners 9 days, then marched out and fired upon & all [killed except for] two or three who escaped by flight. Almost [all] of the Americans from Georgia and Alabama have [died]. The Citizens of Texas are fleeing in every direction; house, farms etc. are deserted and every thing left behind."

UP IN ARMS

As soon as he heard the news, Mirabeau joined the Texas army. The young private soon showed courage under fire. He rescued two Texans who were surrounded by enemy soldiers. The Mexicans were so impressed with his actions, they saluted him on the battlefield! Mirabeau was rewarded for his bravery and leadership. Texas general Sam Houston promoted him to colonel. He also gave Mirabeau command of the cavalry, which was the group of soldiers who fought on horseback.

WHO WAS SAM HOUSTON?

Sam Houston was a great leader, a war hero, and one of the **founding fathers** of Texas. He was born on March 2, 1793, near Lexington Virginia. As a teenager, Houston moved to Tennessee. He grew close to the Cherokee Indians who lived nearby. He later joined the military and eventually served as governor of Tennessee. In March 1836, Houston became major general of the Texas army. He boldly led his men to victory in the Texas Revolution. In September 1836, Houston became the first president of Texas. He returned as president in 1841. He later served as US senator for Texas and governor of the state.

The city of Houston, Texas, is named after Sam Houston.

THE BATTLE OF SAN JACINTO

On April 21, 1836, Mirabeau fought in the Battle of San Jacinto. At 4 p.m., Texas troops attacked a Mexican camp near Harrisburg, Texas. General Sam Houston led the Texas army into battle. Colonel Lamar led the cavalrymen. The Texans surprised the Mexican troops by attacking in broad daylight, while the Mexicans were napping. There were no guards to warn the Mexican soldiers. They were woken by the sound of Texas war cries and the smell of gunpowder.

The Battle of San Jacinto was short but deadly. It lasted just 18 minutes and left 630 Mexican soldiers dead. Another 208 Mexicans were wounded. Only 9 Texans died in the battle. About 730 Mexicans were taken prisoner, including President Santa Anna.

The victory at the Battle of San Jacinto won the revolution for Texas. It also made Mirabeau Lamar a war hero.

POLITICAL REWARDS

Mirabeau's heroism earned him a place in politics. Ten days after the battle, Texas interim president David Burnet made him secretary of war. Mirabeau tried to have Santa Anna executed for killing Texan soldiers. Despite Mirabeau's efforts, though, Santa Anna was allowed to return safely to Mexico. President Burnet also made Mirabeau commander in chief of the Texas army. Mirabeau traveled to Victoria to lead the troops. He was unable to control the rowdy, untrained soldiers, however. Mirabeau left the army and turned his attention back to politics.

Texas Perspective

Mirabeau was a talented leader. He was promoted from private to commander in chief of the Texas army in just 100 days.

From a note Mirabeau wrote to President Burnet on July 17, 1836:

"I have but five minutes to dictate this note to let you know the dreadful state of affairs in the Army. Every thing is in the utmost confusion and rebellion. On my arrival, I was informed that I could not be recognized as commander in chief... I hope I shall be able to recall the old Citizens of Texas to a sense of their rights and their duty..."

David Burnet later became vice president of Texas under President Mirabeau Lamar.

4 TAKING OFFICE

In September 1836, Mirabeau B. Lamar became the first vice president of the Republic of Texas. He served under President Sam Houston. The two men had fought together in the Battle of San Jacinto. Now they would lead the new country together.

DIFFERENT POINTS OF VIEW

Mirabeau was vice president of Texas from 1836 until 1838.

Houston and Mirabeau had very different ideas about Texas, however. President Houston wanted Texas to become part of the United States. Houston also wanted Texans and Indians to live together in peace. Vice President Lamar did not want Texas to join the United States. He thought that Texas should stay independent and expand west to the Pacific Ocean. He also believed that Indians should be driven off of Texas lands.

President Houston was a strong leader with firm beliefs. He had no use for a vice president who did not share his point of view. Over time, the two men became enemies. Mirabeau spent his days as vice president writing poetry, studying Spanish, and traveling. He started to build a plantation called the Oak Grove in Richmond, Texas. Mirabeau also told people about the great new republic and planned how to make it even better.

RUNNING FOR PRESIDENT

In 1838, Mirabeau entered the race for president. Texas law did not allow presidents to serve two terms in a row, so Houston could not run for reelection that year. The people of Texas were eager for change. They welcomed Mirabeau and his new ideas. In a strange turn of events, Mirabeau's first two opponents died before election day. His final opponent was Texas senator Robert Wilson. Wilson entered the race for president just a few days before the election. Mirabeau won by a landslide.

Texas Perspective

Mirabeau became president of a country that had no money and was under constant threat of Indian attacks.

James Collinsworth was one of Mirabeau's two opponents in the 1838 presidential election. Collinsworth was chief justice of the Texas Supreme Court and a signer of the Texas Declaration of Independence.

PRESIDENT LAMAR

On December 10, 1838, Mirabeau B. Lamar was sworn in as the second president of the Republic of Texas. He took control of a country that had many problems. Texas had no money and a lot of debt. Other countries did not see Texas as an independent nation. They would not trade goods with Texas. Indians were attacking the settlers who lived there. Mexico was threatening to invade them, too.

President Lamar believed that Texas could become a great country. He entered office ready to fight for the new republic. When he was sworn in as president, Mirabeau said, "If peace can be obtained only by the sword, let the sword do its work." Mirabeau's first order of business was to make Texas safe for the settlers who lived there.

THE CHEROKEE

In 1839, President Lamar strengthened the Texas **frontier** against Mexican and Indian attacks. He built forts and roads. He hired soldiers to protect the Anglo-American settlers. Then he sent men to negotiate with the Cherokee. The Cherokee were a large and powerful Indian tribe living in eastern Texas. Mirabeau believed the Cherokee were working alongside the Mexicans to take control of Texas. He hoped the Cherokee would leave the country peacefully. However, he was willing to use force to remove them if needed. The Cherokee did not go without a fight. In July 1839, hundreds of Cherokee warriors attacked Texan troops. The Cherokee lost the battle and about 100 men, including their leader Chief Bowl. Texan soldiers burned Cherokee villages and chased the remaining Cherokee into Indian Territory.

After the defeat of the powerful Cherokee, many smaller, peaceful Indian tribes were also forced to leave eastern Texas.

THE COMANCHE

In 1840, President Lamar went to war with the Comanche. The Comanche were a powerful Indian tribe who ruled the plains of central and western Texas. They traveled from place to place to hunt buffalo. Mirabeau wanted the Comanche to leave the plains so Texans could settle there. Mirabeau's soldiers waged war with the Comanche, but the Comanche fought back.

Many homes and lives were lost, but the Comanche refused to leave their land.

From a letter written by President Lamar in May 1839:

"The Cherokees can no longer remain among us...I hope they will go in peace and return no more for we have no wish to shed the blood of the Red men...Should the Cherokees refuse to leave our territory force must be employed."

BUILDING DREAMS

President Lamar had big dreams for Texas. He pictured a country that was orderly, educated, and prosperous. He started to make changes that would grow Texas into a great nation. Mirabeau called for new laws to bring order to the people. He tried to create a national bank to help improve the economy. When that failed, he began to produce Texan money to help lower the country's debt.

TEXAS REDBACKS

The Texas dollar was the new money of Texas. It was called the "Texas redback" because the backs of the bills were red. The Texas government printed the bills from 1839 to 1840. Too many bills were made, however, and the Texas redbacks became almost worthless.

FATHER OF TEXAS EDUCATION

Mirabeau was a scholar who knew the value of education. Within a month of becoming president, he had planned an entire school system for Texas. He set aside large areas of land throughout the country to build public schools and universities. Although the schools were not built for many years, Mirabeau's plans were the basis of the Texas education system.

CAPITAL IDEA

In June 1839, Mirabeau started to build the new capital city of Austin. At the time, the capital was located in the growing city of Houston. Mirabeau moved the capital to an unsettled area of land in the wilderness of central Texas. He chose a spot on the Indian frontier to prove he would continue to expand Texas to the west. Mirabeau's government was moved to Austin in October 1839. At first, the government worked out of log shacks in the woods. Over time, the capital grew into a large, busy city.

Letter from Thomas Jefferson Jones to President Lamar on April 15, 1839, describing the area that would become Austin, Texas:

"It is the most beautiful...scene I ever saw. I know you will be delighted with it...The atmosphere [was] charged with the most delightful perfume and every shrub and every hill and every flower seemed to extend a welcome to the weary traveller...There are hundreds of the most beautiful [sites] for building around the town level...The frontier is now quiet and perfectly safe."

STEPHEN F. AUSTIN

The new capital was named Austin in honor of Stephen F. Austin. Austin had brought many families to Texas and started the first Anglo-American colony there.

Stephen F. Austin is known as the "Father of Texas."

Texas Perspective

Mirabeau moved the Texas capital from Houston to the town of Austin.

FRIENDS OF TEXAS

During his time as president, Mirabeau tried to make peace with Mexico. However, Mexico refused to see Texas as an independent nation. When talks between the two countries failed, President Lamar began to help other people fight Mexico.

Texas Perspective

Mirabeau formed the Texas navy to help Mexican rebels overthrow their government.

YUCATÁN REBELLION

In 1840, the Mexican state of Yucatán declared its independence from Mexico. Mexican ships began blocking Yucatán's ports so it could not trade with other countries. Mexico also threatened to attack Yucatán by sea. President Lamar decided to join Yucatán's fight for freedom. He built up the Texas navy and prepared his ships for battle. In September 1841, Mirabeau allied with Yucatán. He agreed to let Yucatán use three Texas navy ships to defend its coast.

With the help of the Texas navy, Yucatán remained independent for seven years.

SANTA FE EXPEDITION

In June 1841, President Lamar sent 321 men and plenty of goods to Santa Fe. Santa Fe was a northern territory of Mexico and a major trading center. The United States and Mexico traded millions of dollars worth of goods there each year. **Mirabeau** wanted Texas to share the goods and wealth. He also wanted Santa Fe to join Texas. The people of Santa Fe were trying to gain independence from Mexico at the time. **Mirabeau** was eager for them to do so.

The Texas Congress refused to pay for the **expedition**. President Lamar took money for the trip from the government himself. He even traveled with the men on their first day. If the expedition had been a success, **Mirabeau** would have been a hero again. Unfortunately, it was a disaster. The men did not have enough food or water for the long journey. They got lost. Their wagons could not travel over the rugged ground. Indians killed men and stole cattle. It took the weary travelers four months to reach Santa Fe.

When men of the expedition finally reached Santa Fe, the Mexican army marched them to jail in Mexico City. Most were not released from prison until April 1842.

5 STILL FIGHTING

Mirabeau's three-year term as president ended on December 13, 1841. He left Austin and returned to his plantation in Richmond. The failure of the Santa Fe Expedition had turned the public against him. Mirabeau fought to get his good reputation back. He also continued to fight for his country.

ANNEXATION

Mirabeau came to believe that **annexation** would be good for Texas. He thought it would keep the country from coming under British rule. He also thought it would protect slavery, which he strongly supported. Mirabeau traveled from place to place and spoke out in favor of annexation.

On December 29, 1845, Texas became part of the United States. A formal ceremony was held in Texas on February 19, 1846. The United States claimed land near the Rio Grande that had belonged to the Republic of Texas. Mexico did not like the annexation or the United States' claim to the land. In April 1846, Mexican troops crossed the river and killed several American soldiers. This was the start of the Mexican War.

The Mexican army had more than 18,000 troops at the start of the war with the United States in 1846.

MEXICAN WAR

The Mexican War was an armed conflict between Mexico and the United States that lasted from 1846 to 1848. Soldiers fought bloody battles at Palo Alto, Buena Vista, Churubusco, and other places in Mexico. Thousands of men died before the United States captured Mexico City and won the war. On February 2, 1848, the countries signed a peace **treaty** called the Treaty of Guadalupe Hidalgo that gave California, New Mexico, Arizona, and other land to the United States. Mexico also gave up its claim to Texas and the land east of the Rio Grande.

BACK IN BATTLE

Mirabeau joined the US Army to fight in the Mexican War. On September 21, 1846, he saw battle again. Mirabeau and other American soldiers attacked the Mexican city of Monterrey. The Americans had about 6,000 men. The Mexicans had about 9,000 men, good supplies, and a strong position. After three days of hard hand-to-hand combat, the Americans drove the enemy from their forts and homes. The US Army won the battle and Mexico gave up the city. The US considered the aquisition of nearly one-half of Mexico's territory to be **Manifest Destiny**.

Texas Perspective

Mirabeau eventually agreed that allowing the United States to annex Texas was a good idea.

Mirabeau Lamar was promoted to lieutenant colonel for his part in the Battle of Monterrey.

BACK IN OFFICE

Mirabeau returned to politics again, too. He helped form a government in the frontier town of Laredo, Texas. He also commanded the troops there. Mirabeau soon grew restless in the quiet little town, however. In 1847, he was elected to represent Laredo in the Texas State Legislature. He held that position for several years.

A WORTHY MAN

In 1857, Mirabeau published a collection of poetry called *Verse Memorials*. That same year, US president James Buchanan made Mirabeau ambassador to Nicaragua and Costa Rica. Mirabeau worked in those countries for nearly two years until his health began to fail. On December 19, 1859, Mirabeau Buonaparte Lamar died, in his home, at the age of 61. At the time of his death, a Texas newspaper called him a "worthy man."

When the Mexican War ended, Mirabeau began traveling again. In his travels he met a young Texas woman named Henrietta Maffit. The two fell in love and were married in 1851.

From the poem "O Lady, If the Stars So Bright" that Mirabeau wrote for his wife Henrietta before their marriage:

"...thou art dearer to my heart
Than all the gems of earth and
sky; And he who sings thee as thou art,
May boast a song that cannot die.
...blame me not—my skill is gone;
I have no worthy song to give;
But thou shalt be my fav'rite one,
To love and worship while I live;
Whate'er I wander sad and lone,
I will thine angel-image bear
Upon my heart, as on a stone,
In deathless beauty
sculptured there."

6 MIRABEAU'S LEGACY

Mirabeau B. Lamar had big plans and high hopes for Texas. He was a visionary who dreamed of turning the lawless wilderness into a mighty nation. He fought for Texas in war and in the new capital he created. Although his plans sometimes failed, Mirabeau never stopped believing in Texas.

FATHER OF TEXAS EDUCATION

Mirabeau's greatest **legacy** was the Texas education system. Today, many public schools in the state are named after him. Mirabeau once said, "The **cultivated** mind is the guardian genius of democracy." This means that education sets people free. These words became the motto of the University of Texas. Mirabeau Lamar was a great leader who spent his life working for the people of Texas.

Texas Perspective

Mirabeau encouraged Congress to set aside nearly 18,000 acres (7,284 ha) of land in each Texas county for public education.

Lamar University in Beaumont, Texas, is named for Mirabeau.

BIG DREAMER

Mirabeau was a visionary who helped create and shape Texas. A visionary is a person who plans the future with imagination and wisdom. Mirabeau had high hopes and big dreams for the big country. He fought in the capital city and on the battlefields to make those dreams come true.

This monument to Mirabeau Lamar can be found at Stephen F. Austin State University in Nacogdoches, Texas. The inscription reads: "The cultivated mind is the guardian genius of democracy."

This bust of Mirabeau can be found on the campus of Lamar University.

LEARNING MORE

BOOKS

Alter, Judy. *Mirabeau B. Lamar: Second President of Texas*. Abilene, TX: State House Press, 2005.

Wimberley, John. *Life in the Republic of Texas*. Spotlight on Texas. New York: Rosen Classroom, 2010.

WEBSITES

The Handbook of Texas Online
www.tshaonline.org/handbook

Texas Beyond History
www.texasbeyondhistory.net

HISTORIC SITES

The Alamo
www.thealamo.org

Presidio La Bahia
www.presidiolabahia.org

San Jacinto Museum of History
www.sanjacinto-museum.org

Texas Military Forces Museum
www.texasmilitaryforcesmuseum.org/history.htm

TIMELINE

Texas	Mirabeau Lamar

August 16, 1798 Mirabeau Buonaparte Lamar is born near Louisville, Georgia

1819 Moves to Cahawba, Alabama; runs general store and newspaper

1823 Returns to Georgia and becomes secretary to governor

January 1, 1826 Marries Tabitha Jordan; daughter Rebecca Ann is born the next year

1828 Moves to Columbus and starts the *Columbus Enquirer*

1829 Elected to the Georgia Senate

August 20, 1830 Wife Tabitha dies

1832 Runs for Congress but is not elected

1834 Runs for Congress but is not elected

1835 Travels to Texas to recover from brother's death and visit James Fannin; decides to move there

October 2, 1835 Texas Revolution begins with the Battle of Gonzales

March 6, 1836 Mexican army attacks and defeats Texas troops at the Alamo

March 27, 1836 James Fannin and his men are executed in Goliad Massacre

April 1836 Joins Texas Army as a private; quickly promoted to colonel; leads the cavalry at the Battle of San Jacinto

May–June 1836 Named secretary of war in David G. Burnet's cabinet and commander in chief of Texas army

September 1836 Elected first vice president of Texas

December 10, 1838 Sworn in as president of Texas; serves until December 13, 1841

October 1839 The Texas capital is moved to Austin

1843 Daughter Rebecca Ann dies

February 19, 1846 Texas is annexed by the United States

1846 Joins the US Army as inspector general. Fights in the Battle of Monterrey in September and is promoted to lieutenant colonel

1846–1847 Helps form government in Laredo and is elected to represent it in the state legislature

1851 Marries second wife, Henrietta Maffit, and has a daughter named Loretto Evaline

1857 Publishes collection of poems called *Verse Memorials*. US president James Buchanan names him ambassador to Nicaragua and Costa Rica

December 19, 1859 Mirabeau B. Lamar dies in Richmond, Texas

GLOSSARY

ambassador (am-BA-suh-dur) The highest-ranking representative of one country assigned to conduct relations with another country.

annexation (a-nek-SAY-shun) The adding of one piece of territory to another, as the United States annexed Texas in 1845.

Congress (KON-gres) The part of the US government that makes laws and is made of the House of Representatives and the Senate. The members of Congress are chosen by the people of each state.

cultivated (KUL-tih-vayt-ed) Grown and cared for; educated.

defiance (di-FY-unts) Open resistance to authority.

dictator (DIK-tay-ter) One who exercises supreme authority in a country, usually without having been elected to do so.

executed (EK-suh-kyoot-ed) Put to death.

expedition (ek-spuh-DIH-shun) A trip for a special purpose.

founding fathers (FOWND-ing FA-thers) Men who were leading figures in the creation of something, such as a country, an organization, or a group effort to do something.

frontier (frun-TEER) The edge of a settled country, where the wilderness begins.

legacy (LEH-guh-see) Something left behind by a person's actions.

Manifest Destiny (MA-nih-fest DES-tin-ee) Phrase used by US leaders during the 1840s to justify expanding US land holdings.

massacre (MA-sih-ker) The act of killing a large number of people.

negotiate (nih-GOH-shee-ayt) To talk over and arrange terms for an agreement.

politics (PAH-lih-tiks) The science of governments and elections.

prosperous (PROS-per-us) To be successful and wealthy.

reputation (reh-pyoo-TAY-shun) The ideas people have about another person, an animal, or an object.

revolt (rih-VOLT) To fight or rebel.

scholar (SKAH-ler) A person who has gone to school and who has much knowledge.

skirmishes (SKUR-mish-ez) Brief fights or encounters.

treaty (TREE-tee) An official agreement, signed and agreed upon by each party.

tuberculosis (too-ber-kyuh-LOH-sis) A serious infectious disease that affects the lungs.

INDEX